DO NOT REMOVE
CARDS FROM POCKET

SATURN

EXPLORING THE PLANETS

SATURN

Duncan Brewer

MARSHALL CAVENDISH
NEW YORK · LONDON · TORONTO · SYDNEY

Library Edition Published 1992   Allen County Public Library
Ft. Wayne, Indiana

© Marshall Cavendish Limited 1992

Published by Marshall Cavendish Corporation
2415 Jerusalem Avenue
PO Box 587
North Bellmore
New York 11710

Series created by Graham Beehag Book Design
Produced by Marshall Cavendish Corporation

Library of Congress Cataloging-in-Publication Data
Brewer, Duncan, 1938-
    Saturn / Duncan Brewer.
    p. cm. – (Planet guides)
    Includes index.
    Summary: Examines the physical characteristics and conditions of Saturn, describing its position in relation to the sun and other planets and surveying humanity's attempts to penetrate its mysteries.
    ISBN 1-85435-330-6 (set)   ISBN 1-85435-374-8
    1. Saturn (Planet) – Juvenile literature. [1. Saturn (Planet)]
    I. Title. II. Series: Brewer, Duncan, 1938- Planet guides.
    QB671.B74 1990
    523.4'6–dc20
                                                    90-40811
                                                         CIP
                                                          AC

Printed in Singapore by Times Offset Pte Ltd
Bound in the United States by Worzalla Publishing Co.

SAFETY NOTE

Never look directly at the Sun, either with the naked eye or with binoculars or a telescope. To do so can result in permanent blindness.

Acknowledgement
Most of the photographs, maps and diagrams in this book have been kindly supplied by NASA.

Front Page Picture:
**Saturn's rings and it's northern hemisphere are defined by NASA's Voyaager 2 as it approaches the planet.
Voyager 2 was 27,000,000 miles (43,000,000 kilometers) from Saturn when it took this photograph.**

Contents

Planet Saturn and its Family

Saturn was the most distant planet to be recognized by early skywatchers. The earliest written records of Saturn come from Mesopotamia. They go back to 650 B.C. When ancient astronomers gazed at Saturn, they saw a dim body, yellow in color, moving sluggishly. To their eyes, it seemed rather sinister. The astrologers, who

Saturn is seen here at almost its maximum tilt as viewed from Earth, −29° from the vertical.

made predictions about the future based on the movements, relationships and supposed characters of the heavenly bodies, felt that Saturn had an ominous influence that could bring misfortune.

Planet of Fear

The Saturn of Roman myths – Kronos to the Greeks – was a fearsome character. This old, slow-moving man was the father of Jupiter. A prophecy foretold that a son would unseat Saturn from his throne. So, Saturn ate his children in an attempt to avoid his fate. However, Jupiter's mother saved her son from the cannibalistic old man. Eventually, Jupiter – Zeus in Greek mythology – deposed his father, as predicted.

The word saturnine means, "glowering and malevolent." The medieval astrologers thought the planet Saturn was slow and heavy. They associated it with the metal lead. Eventually, the grim old man of Greek and Roman myth became portrayed as Old Father Time. This long-bearded figure with an hourglass and scythe slowly but inevitably moves through our lives. He will reap us like ripe wheat when our time is up.

Astrologers considered Saturn a male planet with the characteristics of Earth and lead, and with the properties of dry and cold. Agriculture, the elderly and the melancholic came under its protection.

7

Lazy Traveler

Saturn's slow journey around the Sun takes 29 years 167 days of Earth time. It moves lazily across the night sky, relative to the positions of the stars, so it is always easy to find. It remains within each of the 12 constellations of the *zodiac* for about 2 ½ years.

The angle of Saturn's orbit is small, just 2°. Earth and Saturn come into *opposition*, forming a straight line with the Sun, once every 378·09 days. Therefore, every Earth year, the opposition occurs about thirteen days later than the year before. Excellent viewing conditions for astronomers studying Saturn from Earth occur for several months of the year.

Giant Revealed

Modern viewing techniques, both from Earth and from space probes, reveal a far different planet to the murky disk seen in earlier days. We now know that Saturn is a huge planet of great beauty. Its flattened, glowing orb is encircled with shining rings and has a large family of moons.

Taken at a distance of 1,768,422 miles (2,845,922 kilometers), this Pioneer 11 picture clearly shows the planet's ring system as well as its major moon, Titan.

Discovering the Planet

The pioneering Italian astronomer, Galileo Galilei, first pointed his early home-made telescope in the direction of Saturn in 1610. He was surprised to see what he thought were two large moons. He saw one on each side of the planet. These "moons" appeared to flank Saturn symmetrically. They seemed so large that Galileo concluded that he had discovered some sort of triple

9

planet. His telescope had a *magnification* of only 32, and the image he saw through the imperfectly ground lenses of the time was not very sharp. He wrote that Saturn was not alone in space, but "is composed of three bodies which almost touch one another." He felt that the central planet was "about three times the size of the lateral ones."

Galileo described the apparent moons as "two servants helping old, slow Saturn on its way." He was puzzled because the two "lateral" bodies did not act at all like the sort of moons he had already observed rotating around Jupiter. These moons appeared to stay still, one on each side of Saturn.

Galileo's Confusion

Two years later, in 1612, Galileo was even more puzzled to discover that the odd moons of Saturn had totally disappeared. He wondered whether perhaps Saturn, true to its mythological reputation, had devoured its children. In frustration, he wrote that "the unexpected nature of the event, the weakness of my understanding, and the fear of being wrong, have confounded me greatly."

This montage of Voyager 1 and 2 photographs shows Saturn and seven of its satellites. The ruddy-orange moon at top right is Titan. Clockwise from it are Iapetus, Tethys, Mimas, Enceladus, Dione, and Rhea.

Tilted View

Modern astronomers understand the reason for Galileo's confusion. In 1610, the planet's tilt, in relation to its position as seen from Earth, had allowed him to see its rings, but dimly. They were visible as narrow extensions on both sides of the main planet. In 1612, however, Saturn's equator was much more in line with his field of vision. The rings, which are only a mile or so thick, were edge-on as seen from Earth. They were therefore completely invisible to his crude telescope.

Brink of Discovery

By 1616, Galileo could see the rings once more. This time, they presented a wider expanse than in 1610. He now perceived the rings as "two half ellipses." But he was still unable to understand the true nature and structure of the broad band circling the planet. Sveral drawings of Saturn in letters to freinds showed that Galileo had been getting close to an accurate portrayal of the ring system. But, like other astronomers at the time, his mind seemed unable to grasp a phenomenon so different from anything that had ever been observed before. It was not a part of his visual vocabulary. Galileo died in 1642 without discovering the true identity of the strange "half-ellipses."

Monster Telescopes

The telescopes used by Galileo were quite small. They were designed to be held, balanced on a windowsill, or attached to a small stand. As telescope technology improved, the instruments became larger and longer. By 1650, telescopes more than 150 feet (50 meters) in length had been built. Hevelius, a Polish astronomer, had one of these cumbersome monsters. It needed a hoist to set it into position. Using such instruments,

Hevelius and others, including Langrenus from Belgium, and Riccioli and Grimaldi from Italy, attempted to make the first maps of the Moon. A growing number of European scientists were now trying to solve the problem of Saturn's unusual shape. In the 1650s, they came up with a wide range of drawings. Some of them were quite accurate, yet none of these Saturn-observers realized that they were dealing with a wide ring circling the planet's equator.

Rings and Satellites

It was a Dutch astronomer, Christiaan Huygens, who made the breakthrough. In 1659, he published a paper, entitled *Systema Saturnium,* which described his work over the previous four years. Huygens wrote in code like all cautious men of science in those days. He revealed the true nature of Saturn's rings: "Saturn is surrounded by a thin, flat ring, not adhering to the planet at any point, and inclined to the ecliptic." Huygens had been able to make his discovery using an excellent telescope with a magnification of 50. He was also the first man to discover a true moon of Saturn; he found Titan in 1655.

Early astronomers had no idea that Saturn could display such sharp divisions of light and shadow. Voyager was able to view the planet from below, with the light of the Sun shining through the rings, and bringing the ring particles into strong focus. A starry background has been added to this Voyager image.

Giovanni Domenico Cassini. In the background is the Paris Observatory of which he was director for many years.

Giovanni Domenico Cassini was the first director of the then new Paris Observatory. In 1675, he discovered a break in Saturn's ring. It completely divided the ring into the outer and inner portions now known as the A Ring and B Ring respectively. This gap, which is about 2,500 miles (4,000 kilometers) wide, is known as the *Cassini Division* in honor of its discoverer. The discovery of a break in the ring placed doubt on the theories that Saturn's ring might be one single solid or liquid entity.

Moon Hunting

Cassini was an enthusiastic Saturn watcher. He had already discovered two more satellites of the planet, Iapetus in 1671, and Rhea in 1672. He used a refracting telescope, with a small *aperture* and a very long *focal length*. All early telescopes were refracting telescopes. They had an eyepiece lens nearest the eye and an *objective lens* at the other end. The light-gathering diameter of the objective lens is called the aperture.

Cassini discovered the satellites of Saturn with a refracting telescope whose objective lens was placed high on a balcony, facing roughly in the right direction. The eyepiece was some 90 feet (27 meters) below, at ground level. It consisted of a magnifying glass with which the astronomer hunted the desired image.

Tubeless Lenses

Cassini's refracting telescope had no tube connecting the objective with the eyepiece. It was known as an *air telescope.* The great length of the single lens refractor telescopes was designed to reduce the effect known as

The rings of Saturn cast their shadow onto the planet's equatorial region in this Pioneer picture, taken at a distance of 1,500,000 miles (2,415,000 kilometers). The Cassini Division is clearly seen separating the outer and inner rings.The moon Rhea orbits close below the planet.

chromatic aberration. This results in the presence of bright, false colors in the image. Chromatic aberration is caused by the way light behaves when it passes through a simple single lens. Nowadays these false colors are eliminated by using compound lenses of different materials and various curvatures. Such lenses are known as *achromatic lenses* or *apochromatic lenses*.

In 1684, using a massive air telescope with a focal length of about 130 feet (40 meters), Cassini discovered two more satellites of Saturn, now known as Dione and Tethys.

Rings Within Rings

Modern images show that Saturn's ring is made up of a huge number of individual concentric rings. They look like a long-playing record or a compact disk. In 1837, the Director of the Berlin Observatory, Johann Franz Encke, discovered a black line in the A Ring, about a third of the way out from the inner edge. Known as the Encke Division, it divides regions of slightly differing brightness.

In 1850, a darker, less well-defined ring was discovered between the B Ring and the planet. Now known as the C Ring, it was discovered by an American team at the Harvard College Observatory headed by

Showing Saturn's rings from a viewpoint directly over the planet's north pole, this computer image lays out the ring system in a multiple band extending 48,000 miles (77,000 kilometers) from the planet's cloud tops.

William Bond. The C Ring is so transparent that it is sometimes possible to see stars through it. It is also known as the Crêpe or Pancake Ring.

Settling the Argument

At the time that the C Ring was discovered, there were many conflicting arguments about the structure of the rings. William Bond and others thought they might be liquid. To try to settle the matter, Cambridge University,

Saturn's A Ring is 9,300 miles (15,000 kilometers) wide and has a dark band, the narrow Encke Division, near its outer edge. The Cassini Division, which separates the outer A-ring from the inner B-ring, shows blue in the bottom right of this false-color image.

Seen from a distance of 445,500 miles (717,000 kilometers) in this Voyager picture, the wide rings of Saturn are clearly made up of countless smaller rings, packed together like grooves on a compact disk.

in England, held a contest. The winner would be the scientist who could establish most convincingly whether rings with the stability and appearance of those around Saturn were more likely to be rigid, liquid, or partly made of gases.

In 1857, the brilliant physicist, James Clerk-Maxwell won the prize. He demonstrated that the rings could not be solid, liquid, or made of gas, but must consist of a huge number of small paticles. Clerk-Maxwell also proved mathematically that a solid ring would inevitably be broken up by the forces exerted on it.

Revolving Rings

We know now that the rings of Saturn are made up of millions of fragments of ice and maybe rock, ranging from the size of pebbles to the size of a small house. The closer the rings are to Saturn, the faster they orbit it. In

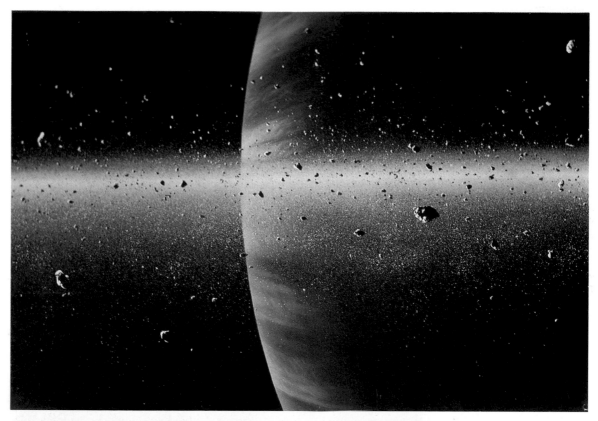

Above: The ice particles that make up Saturn's rings vary in size from tiny gravel-like fragments to hunks as large as houses. Seen edge-on, the rings may be no thicker than 300 feet (90 meters).

Left: The darkest band here, divided by narrow white strips, is the shadow cast on the planet's cloud layer by the rings, which can be seen toward the bottom right of the image. North of the shadow, huge pale atmospheric features are shaped by the 1,000 mph (1,800 km/h) winds of Saturn's equatorial jet-stream.

1895, scientists used spectroscopes, and calculations based on the *Doppler Effect*, to work out the speed of the icy particles in the rings. They discovered that those at the inner edge of the B Ring travel at 9·8 miles (18·9 kilometers) per second. Those at the outer edge of the A Ring travel at 11·8 miles (15·8 kilometers) per second. It takes fragments at the inner edge of the C Ring 5·6 hours to complete a circuit around the planet. At the outer edge of the A Ring, the period is 14·2 hours.

The Roche Limit

The rings of Saturn fit neatly into a region known as the *Roche Limit,* named after the mid-nineteenth century mathematician, Edouard Roche, who calculated its presence and size. Roche worked out that every planet has a zone around it within which the force of the planet's gravity is strong enough to break up bodies intruding from space. Very strong solid bodies are not

Illustrated with the Earth, and shown to the same scale, the rings of Saturn dwarf our planet with their width. Yet they are so thin that they seem to disappear when viewed edge-on through most earth-bound telescopes.

affected, but bodies with a looser construction, such as ice, or conglomerations of rocky fragments, are pulled apart. In most cases this extends outward to about 2·4 times the planet's radius from the planet's center. Roche argued that Saturn's rings were probably formed from fragments of intruding bodies, such as asteroids and comets, destroyed within the Roche Limit.

Planet Leftovers

Planets are generally thought to have formed after the birth of the Sun, when accumulations of gas and cosmic particles gradually came together into spheres orbiting the new star. The major planets grew by mopping up many smaller orbiting bodies after pulling them in with their superior gravitational forces. One popular theory is that the rings of Saturn are composed of material left

This spectacular picture of the rings of Saturn was taken by Voyager 1 in November 1980. The picture clearly shows the thin shadow on the surface of the planet cast by the rings.

over from the formation of the planet, and that the orbiting fragments were unable, for some reason, to combine with the other material that forms the planet itself. Also, because the ring material is within the Roche Limit, it has been unable to form itself into an icy satellite, owing to the disruptive force of Saturn's gravity.

The Seven Rings

In all, Saturn has seven named rings of varying widths and brightness. They are lettered according to the order in which they were discovered. Starting at the planet and working outward, the first is the faint D Ring. It begins at the top of the planet's atmosphere and extends 8,700 miles (14,000 kilometers) to the C Ring.

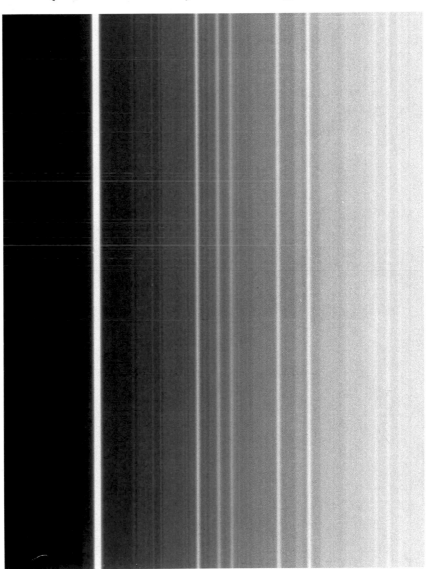

From Earth, we can see only the three main rings of Saturn, but this Voyager image of a section of the rings confirms that the entire ring system is made up of a large number of ringlets.

The C Ring, 11,000 miles (18,000 kilometers) wide, reflects sunlight, but observers can see the planet through it.

Next comes the B Ring, which is 15,500 miles (25,000 kilometers) wide, and the brightest and densest of all the rings. It is followed by a gap, called the Cassini Division, 2,000 miles (3,500 kilometers) wide.

The A Ring is next and is 15,000 kilometers (9,300 miles) wide. Within it is the 223-mile (360-kilometer) wide Encke Division.

The narrow F Ring is 2,480 miles (4,000 kilometers) beyond the outer edge of the A Ring. It is only 62 miles (100 kilometers) across. The Voyager probes showed that it has several strands, which are unevenly interwined, with occasional "knots" which may indicate

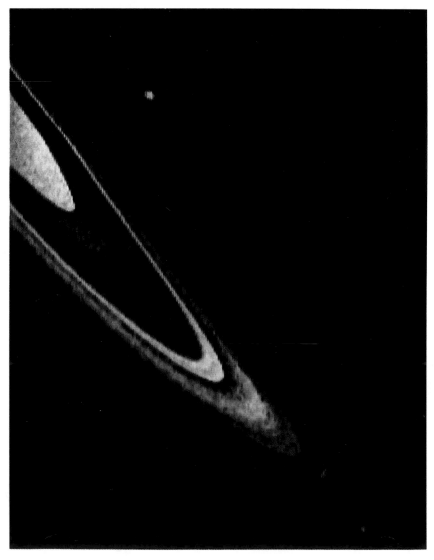

Pioneer 11 greatly increased our knowledge of Saturn's rings. It revealed for the first time the faint outline of the F Ring and discovered new moons, including Atlas, visible here at the bottom right of the picture. Another of Saturn's moons, Tethys, is visible above the rings.

the presence of small satellites. Two known satellites, Prometheus and Pandora, orbit Saturn close to the F Ring, one on each side, and their gravitational fields may have something to do with the strange braiding of the ring's strands.

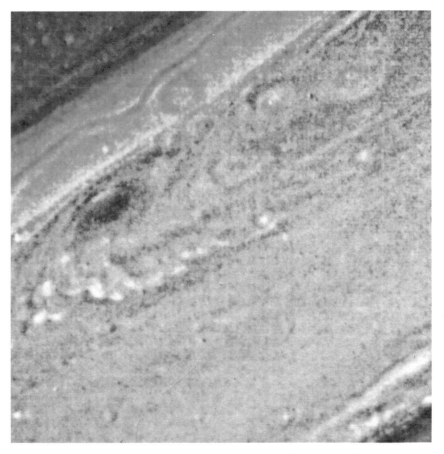

The F Ring is more than 49,600 miles (80,000 kilometers) from Saturn. Another 18,600 miles (30,000 kilometers) out in space is the slender G Ring, and 24,800 miles (40,000 kilometers) beyond that is the beginning of the E Ring. This is the outermost region of the planet's ring system. The E Ring is faint and is 55,800 miles (90,000 kilometers) broad. Several satellites orbit Saturn within the E Ring.

It is possible that the widely spread material of the E Ring is constantly fed with particles from the moon Enceladus, which orbits within the ring. The particles could spray out into the ring as a result of tiny *micrometeorites* bombarding Enceladus, or they might be material that has been thrown up from beneath the moon's surface.

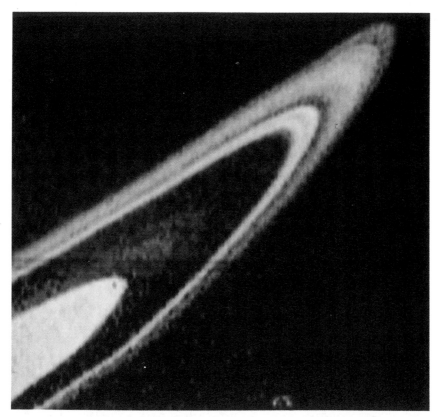

Left: Tethys, one of Saturn's moons, can just be seen at the bottom of this Pioneer 11 image of the planet's ring system. Tethys was discovered in 1684 by Giovanni Domenico Cassini. It consists of at least 50 percent ice and orbits Saturn at a distance of over 183,000 miles (295,000 kilometers).

Below: In this artist's impression, Voyager has moved behind and below Saturn's rings to take pictures of sunlight shining through the rings, highlighting the particles of which they are formed.

The Gas Giants

Jupiter, Saturn, Uranus and Neptune are known as the gas giants. Unlike Mercury, Venus, Earth and Mars, which are known as the terrestrial planets, the gas giants consist mainly of gases, though sometimes the gases exist in forms that are never found on Earth.

Saturn is the second largest gas giant. It orbits the Sun at a *mean distance* of about 885,000,000 miles (1,427,000,000 kilometers). This makes it the flattest of all the planets. Scientists call flatness *oblateness,* and they have worked out a formula for measuring it. The polar diameter is subtracted from the equatorial

A close-up of the orange outer edge of the A Ring. The black region is the inner edge of Ecke's Division, and the red strands are the components of a ringlet that lies inside the Ecke's Division.

SATURN

EARTH

JUPITER

The gas giants Jupiter and Saturn are the two largest planets in the Solar System, with diameters of 88,733 miles (142,800 kilometers) and 74,978 miles (120,660 kilometers) respectively. In this montage, we can see them dwarfing a tiny Earth, with its diameter of only 7,927 miles (12,757 kilometers).

diameter, and the result is divided by the equatorial diameter. Using this formula, the oblateness of Saturn is 0·1, making the planet much flatter than Earth, which has an oblateness of 0·0034, far smaller than Saturn's.

The reason that Saturn is so flat is that it spins very fast. This makes it bulge outward around its middle The planet spins arond once every 10 hours 14 minutes at its equator. At the poles, the rotation period is 10 hours 40 minutes. The difference occurs because the planet is not one solid lump, like Earth. Most of its structure consists of gases and liquids, with its solid core deep in its center. This causes these varying speeds of surface spin, which are known as differential rotation.

The inclination of Saturn's axis of rotation is steep — about 26°·5. This alternately tilts its northern and southern hemispheres toward the Sun, causing seasons, as on Earth.

Saturn is 750 times larger than Earth. However, the amount of matter — the mass — that makes up this volume is comparatively small and this gives Saturn the lowest density of all the planets. While Earth's density is 5·5 times that of water, Saturn's density is only 0·69 of the density of water. If the planet could be dropped into a gigantic sea, it would float.

At the center of all four gas giants is a rocky core. Saturn's core is about the same size as that of Earth, but it has a far greater mass, with perhaps ten times as much material as there is in the Earth crammed into about the same volume. This core is under a pressure of about 8,000,000 Earth atmospheres and has a temperature of about 22,000°F (12,000°C).

Most of Saturn's bulk and atmosphere consists of hydrogen. We usually think of hydrogen as being a gas, but under certain circumstances, such as very high pressure, it can also be a liquid. Around Saturn's core is a layer of hydrogen under such extremes of heat and pressure that it has become a liquid. It also

Did You Know?
Saturn is composed mostly of hydrogen and helium gas and liquid, like Jupiter. But it is smaller than Jupiter. It has the lowest density of all the planets in the Solar System.

has certain characteristics usually associated with metals, such as the ability to allow heat to flow through it very efficiently. For this reason, it is called metallic liquid hydrogen. This layer is about 8,700 miles (14,000 kilometers) thick.

Metallic Fields

The way in which planets acquire a magnetic field is not fully understood, but scientists believe it has something to do with the presence of metallic liquids in the planet's interior. The Earth's magnetic field is created by currents in its outer core of liquid nickel-iron, which surrounds the solid inner core. Similarly, Saturn's powerful magnetic field, discovered by the Pioneer and Voyager probes, is believed to be due to movements in the planet's metallic liquid hydrogen layer.

Outside the layer of metalic liquid hydrogen is another layer of hydrogen, which is also under such great pressure that it is a liquid. This is a particular form of hydrogen known as molecular hydrogen. The molecular liquid hydrogen layer of Saturn is about 18,600 miles (30,000 kilometers) thick. As the pressure on it decreases, toward its outer region, it gradually becomes gaseous hydrogen. This change-over marks the beginning of Saturn's atmosphere.

Hydrogen Atmosphere

Hydrogen makes up 92·4 percent of Saturn's atmosphere, and helium makes up 7·4 percent. These are the ancient gases stemming from the time of the planet's formation with the rest of the Solar System 4,500,000,000 years ago. There are also small amounts of other gases. Methane and ammonia have been detected, and there are minute traces of acetylene and hydrogen cyanide. Saturn's atmospheric envelope extends over 625,000 miles (1,000,000 kilometers) beyond the visible planet.

Satur's rings cast an enormous shadow on the planet's sunlit side. The pale band in the planet's northern latitudes marks a jet-stream wind that circles Saturn at a speed of about 330 mph (530 km/h). Just underneath it, the pale cloud shapes of gigantic atmospheric storms can be seen.

29

The shadow of Saturn's rings, striking the planet's equatorial zone, displays two fine lines of light where the sun's rays have passed through the relatively particle-free bands between the major rings.

Both Jupiter and Saturn radiate more heat energy than they receive from the Sun, but for different reasons. Jupiter radiates twice as much energy as it receives. The extra heat emission comes from heat left over from the time the planets were forming. As they mopped up material around them, they also contracted, pulling the material in tighter. Contraction always produces heat, and Jupiter is still radiating some of this original heat. It continues to contract slightly, perhaps a millimeter each year, which also adds to the heat emission.

Saturn radiates three times as much heat energy as it receives. It was never as hot as Jupiter in the first place, and it has had plenty of time to cool down in the last 4,500,000,000 years. Information from the Pioneer and Voyager probes shows that Saturn has a smaller

Voyager 2 leaves Earth aboard its Titan Centaur-7 rocket carrier, roaring away from Cape Canaveral at 10:29 a.m. on August 20, 1977, to be followed by Voyager 1 on September 5 the same year. They reached Saturn in November 1980 (Voyager 1) and August 1981 (Voyager 2).

proportion of helium in its atmosphere than Jupiter, though both started with the same mixture of hydrogen and helium.

Scientists have calculated that Saturn's internal temperature has dropped faster than Jupiter's. About 2,000,000,000 years ago, Saturn's internal temperature fell to the level at which helium began to condense on to the outer surface of the metallic liquid hydrogen zone of the planet. The droplets of helium, being denser than liquid hydrogen, began to fall in a "helium rain" toward the planet's core. The motion of the inward-falling helium creates heat-energy, which the

31

planet eventually radiates. This explains both the lower proportion of helium in Saturn's atmosphere, and the higher level of its radiated heat-energy.

Twice as far from the Sun as Jupiter, Saturn has a colder outer atmosphere. It also has a weaker gravity — 1·15 times as strong as Earth's, compared to Jupiter's 2·64 times as strong. Saturn has similar cloud layers to Jupiter, but because of its weaker gravity, they are much deeper, and the thick outer layer evenly masks the planet's sphere.

The outer cloud layer consists of ammonia crystals and forms a dense envelope around the planet at altitudes of between 75 and 100 miles (120 and 160 kilometers).

Resembling a ringed planet seen from above its north pole, this gold-plated copper disc was carried in Voyager 2. It contained two hours of sounds, music, and digital data, on the chance it might one day be discovered by intelligent beings somewhere in space.

The Voyager spacecraft was dominated by a high-gain antenna with a diameter of 13 feet (4 meters). Its radio isotope thermo-electric generators were attached to a long beam, while the sensitive imaging equipment was situated on a gantry at the other end of the spacecraft to minimize radiation interference from the generators.

Below this, at altitudes of between 30 and 45 miles (50 and 70 kilometers), there is another thick barrier made of ammonium hydrosulfide crystals. Below this, from an altitude of about 12½ miles (20 kilometers) down to the outer surface of the liquid molecular hydrogen region of the planet, there is possibly, a layer of clouds made up of water crystals.

It is difficult to see detail on Saturn. Thick hazes in its upper atmosphere obscure detail. These hazes are *photochemical smogs*, similar to the hazes that hang over large cities on Earth. Earth smog is caused by the action of sunlight on vehicle exhaust fumes. Around Saturn they result from the reaction of sunlight with naturally occurring gases, high above the planet.

Voyager 2 penetrated the hazes with its cameras and showed that Saturn's clouds are divided into wide zones around the planet, shaped by strong winds. On Earth, winds are caused when air is warmed by the heat of the Sun reflected from the planet's surface. The warm air rises, and colder air rushes to fill its place. The heat that causes the winds on Saturn comes from within the planet. The heat of the Sun is very weak because of the enormous distance of Saturn from the Sun.

Pioneer 11 flew close enough to Jupiter to allow a gravity-assisted deflection to send it on its 5-year journey to Saturn. The Pioneer probes were pathfinders for the later, more sophisticated Voyager missions.

Saturn has a powerful wind called the *equatorial jet*, which races around the planet at a headlong 800 mph (1,300 km/h) between the latitudes of 40° North and 40° South. Beyond these latitudes, a sudden and substantial drop in wind speed, marked with swirling eddies of cloud, occurs.

Beneath the hazes, Saturn is also revealed to have large spots in its cloud layers, of varying shades of brown, white and red. The largest, nicknamed Big Bertha, is a reddish oval cloud at 72° North, measuring 6,000 by 3,700 miles (10,000 by 6,000 kilometers). At 42° North, the Voyager pictures also revealed three brown spots, the largest of which measures 2,000 by 3,000 miles (3,300 by 5,000 kilometers).

Color from the Depths

In the planet's southern hemisphere, the Voyager cameras picked up a red spot 1,900 by 3,000 miles (3,000 by 5,000 kilometers), at a latitude of about 55° South. Like the Great Red Spot on Jupiter, this spot on Saturn, nicknamed Anne's Spot in honor of the technician who first saw it, probably gets its ruddy color from red phosphorous. This hue is created by the effect of ultraviolet solar rays on the gas phosphine, which is brought up from the depths of the planet's atmosphere by powerful convection currents.

In addition to the relatively stable giant spots, Saturn's cloud systems also contain unstable storm features, such as hurricanes, and cloud shapes formed by the jet stream. They may last only a week or two before they disperse. They may be geared to the violent convection forces active throughout Saturn's atmosphere, which produce strong vertical movements, including cylinders or convection "towers" that help to power the mighty winds.

First Close Look

Pioneer 11, launched from Cape Canaveral on April 6, 1973, a year after Pioneer 10, flew past Jupiter in

December, 1974. Pioneer 11 came close to Jupiter, and the controllers back on Earth were able to use the strong pull of Jupiter's gravity to help change the space-probe's course, sending it on its way toward Saturn. While Pioneer 10 headed irretrievably out into space, Pioneer 11 doubled back across the Solar System. After a journey of almost five years, it closed in on Saturn's orbit in September, 1979. Pioneer 11 discovered Saturn's F Ring and made the first close examination of the planet's magnetosphere and radiation belts. In 1977, the more sophisticated Voyager probes were launched. They reached Jupiter in March, and July, 1979, and both of them used gravity-assisted boosts from Jupiter to speed them toward Saturn. They arrived there in November, 1980, and August, 1981.

Did You Know?

Saturn's rings are very thin compared to their 171,000 miles (275,000 km) diameter. They are only about 300 feet (100 meters) thick. On this scale, a long-playing record 0.06 in (1·5 mm) thick would be 2·5 miles (4 km) across.

Probing the Layers

The two Voyagers looked closely at Saturn's weather system and made breathtaking new pictures of the rings. Using special cameras and filters, they were able to make clear pictures of the cloud layers, penetrating the hazes and identifying the different chemicals making up the layers. They also showed the composition of the rings and discovered Saturn's roaring equatorial winds.

Wheel of Ice

Voyager 1 sent back the first images of a new phenomenon that takes the form of shadowy "spokes" running across the disk of the rings. They radiate outward like the spokes of a wheel and rotate with the planet. From one side of the rings, the spokes appeared dark. However, when Voyager 1 viewed them from the other side, the spokes gleamed brightly. This showed that they are almost certainly made of ice crystals. In some way, the planet's magnetic field has marshalled the tiny ice crystals into their revolving, spoke-like pattern.

Pioneer 11 reached a speed of 100,000 mph (160,000 km/h) after being deflected by Jupiter's gravity field. Here, we can see it closing on Saturn, where it studied the planet's magnetosphere and radiation belts. Pioneer 11 also discovered the narrow outer F Ring.

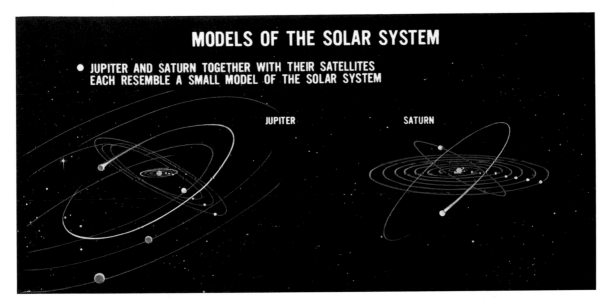

MODELS OF THE SOLAR SYSTEM

● JUPITER AND SATURN TOGETHER WITH THEIR SATELLITES
EACH RESEMBLE A SMALL MODEL OF THE SOLAR SYSTEM

JUPITER   SATURN

Above: With their families of orbiting moons, Jupiter and Saturn are like Solar Systems in miniature, though neither planet radiates heat-energy as the Sun does.

Left: Saturn's inner C Ring, appearing blue in this false-color image, begins about 8,700 miles (14,000 kilometers) from the planet. Outside the G Ring, which is 11,000 miles (18,000 kilometers) across, the B Ring begins, (colored yellow here), in which the ring material is much more densely packed.

Snowballs in Space

Experiments carried out by the Voyager spacecraft studied the fragments that make up the rings. The probes beamed out radio waves and measured the way the ring particles scattered solar rays. They confirmed that the rings still contain particles in a wide variety of sizes. The sizes are not necessarily constant. It is likely that these icy particles are constantly binding together like snowballs. They probably become larger and larger, and then break down again as they collide with one another or are pulled apart by the tidal forces exerted by the planet's gravity.

Saturn has more moons or satellites than any other planet in the Solar System. The Voyager probes were able to make the first close studies of them, and they discovered many new ones.

Massive Titan

Chief by far of Saturn's moons, and the first to be discovered, is Titan. Aptly named, Titan is second in size to Jupiter's Ganymede as a Solar System satellite. It is truly planet-sized, larger than Mercury. Christiaan Huygens discovered Titan on March 25, 1655, using a refracting telescope with a magnification of 50.

Titan orbits Saturn at an average distance of 760,000 miles (1,221,800 kilometers). It takes nearly 16 days to complete each almost circular orbit.

Titan has a diameter of more than 3,000 miles (5,000 kilometers). Voyager 1 came within 4,000 miles (6,500 kilometers) of it during its fly-by. Using infrared and ultraviolet sensors, Voyager determined that Titan has a dense atmosphere consisting mainly of nitrogen. Except for our own planet Earth, Titan is the only other body in the Solar System with a nitrogen-rich atmosphere. Titan also has methane in its atmosphere, and trace elements of other hydrocarbons such as propane, ethylene, and acetylene.

Voyager 1 discovered no appreciable magnetic field around Titan. Titan's density is almost twice that of water, and it is probably composed of roughly equal proportions of rock and ice, with an icy mantle over a rocky core. The satellite has a surface pressure of about 1,500 millibars, one and a half times that of Earth.

| Moon | Distance from Saturn | | Approximate Length of Day | Year Discovered |
	100 mi	100km		
Atlas	(86)	138	0·6	1980
Prometheus	(87)	139	0·6	1980
Pandora	(89)	142	0·6	1980
Janus	(94)	151	0·7	1980
Epimetheus	(94)	151	0·7	1980
Mimas	(115)	185	0·9	1789
Enceladus	(148)	238	1·4	1789
Tethys	(183)	295	1·9	1684
Telesto	(183)	295	1·9	1980
Calypso	(183)	295	1·9	1980
Pan	(183)	295	1·9	1990
Dione	(234)	377	2·7	1684
Helene	(234)	377	2·7	1980
Rhea	(327)	527	4·5	1672
Titan	(760)	1,222	16	1655
Hyperion	(920)	1,481	21	1848
Iapetus	(2,213)	3,561	79	1671
Phoebe	(8,049)	12,954	550	1898

Right: In this artist's impression of Saturn as seen from the surface of Titan, the planet's ring system shows itself to be wafer-thin when viewed edge-on. Titan has a thick crust of water-ice over an inner core of rock.

Seas of Methane

Titan has no magnetic field, so it probably does not have the sort of conductive liquid metal inner layer that produces a dynamo effect in Jupiter and Saturn. Titan's surface temperature is around −292°F (−180°C). It is cold enough to condense methane in the moon's atmosphere, causing it to rain down, and maybe even to form methane "oceans." Unfortunately, the Voyager probes could produce no visible-light pictures of Titan's surface through the density of the red-orange clouds that mask the huge satellite.

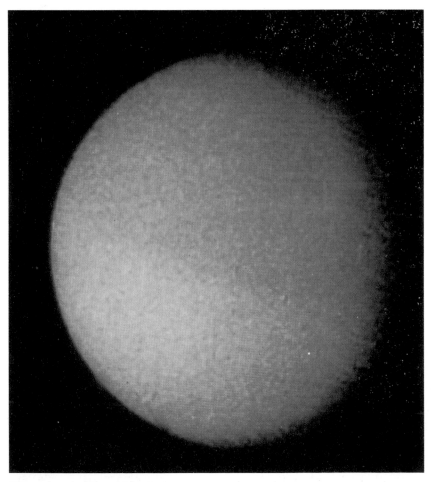

Voyager 1 came very close to Titan, taking this picture at a distance of only 4,350 miles (7,000 kilometers). Titan has an atmosphere mainly of nitrogen and is constantly wrapped in an orange haze.

Frozen Evolution

Of all the known bodies in the Solar System, Titan is the one most likely to evolve the conditions that allowed life to develop on Earth. It has the right sort of atmosphere, mainly nitrogen. The space probes have discovered trace elements in its atmosphere, such as hydrogen cyanide, which were the raw material of life

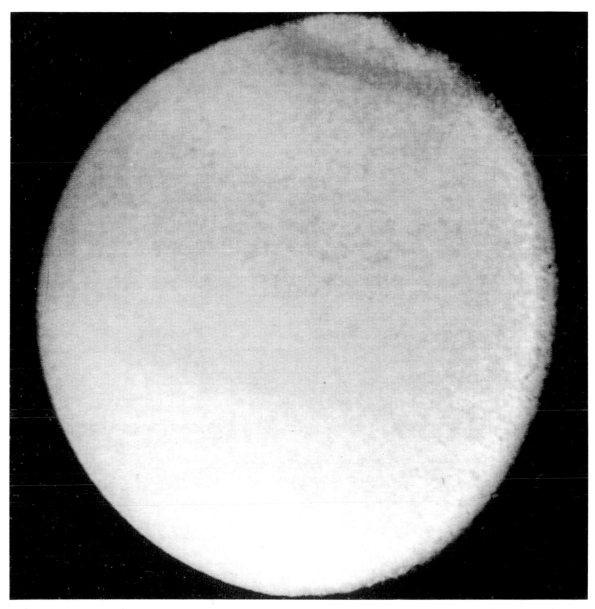

This Voyager image reveals a dark ring around the moon's northern polar region. Titan may experience seasonal differences, which could account for the differing brightnesses of its northern and southern hemispheres.

on Earth. Ultraviolet radiation from the Sun and energy from Saturn's magnetosphere, could play a part in breaking down old elements and creating new ones. At present, Titan's low temperature has frozen the development at a stage comparable to pre-life conditions on Earth.

The First Nine Moons

Unlike Titan, most of Saturn's "classic" moons are composed mainly of ice, possibly with small rocky components. In addition to Titan, the named moons are Iapetus, Rhea, Dione and Tethys (discovered in the

1600s), Mimas and Enceladus (discovered in 1789), Hyperion (1848) and Phoebe (1898). The remaining moons Atlas, Prometheus, Pandora, Janus, Epimetheus, Telesto, Calypso, Helene and Pan were discovered as a result of Voyager's fly-by of Saturn in 1980. More moons were identified amongst the rings but their orbits are as yet unknown and they remain unnamed.

Far Phoebe

In 1848, William Bond, an American astronomer who discovered the C Ring two years later, sighted a satellite which was also seen, later that same year, by British astronomer William Lassell in England. Lassell named the new moon Hyperion. Fifty years later, in 1898, another American, W. H. Pickering, photographing Saturn from an observatory in Peru, discovered Phoebe. It is the most distant of the planet's moons, orbiting 8,047,000 miles (12,950,000 kilometers) from the planet once every 550 days. Its direction is the opposite to all the other satellites, or retrograde.

New Moons

Eighty years passed between the discovery of Phoebe

Titan may have developed its atmosphere, seen here as a blue haze, from gases such as nitrogen and methane trapped in its icy mantle, which were later released during a period of increased temperature.

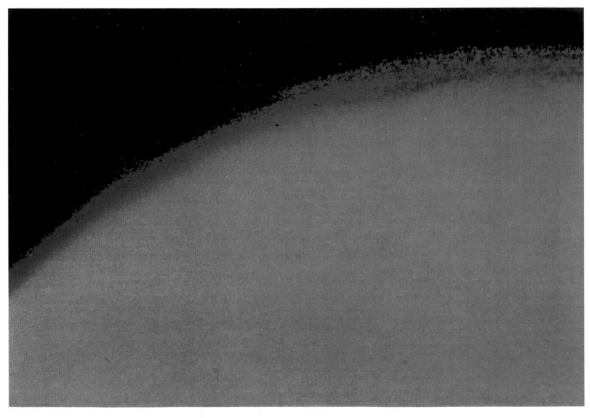

Did You Know?
The pressure in the middle layer of Saturn's three-layer structure, between the rocky core and liquid outer layer, is equivalent to three million Earth atmospheres.

and the confirmation of new satellites. The most recent discoveries are very small compared to the "classic" moons. They are very difficult to see except when the rings tilt toward Earth, which occurs only once every 15 to 17 years. Most of the new satellites have been added to the list from Pioneer and Voyager sightings.

Five of the new satellites, Atlas, Prometheus, Pandora, Janus and Epimetheus, orbit Saturn inside the orbit of Mimas. Others are *co-orbital* with some of the named moons. Mimas, Tethys, and Dione are all known to share their orbits with one or more co-orbiting satellites. When this happens, the smaller satellites circle the planet at a distance of 60° from the larger bodies whose orbit they share.

Keeping their Place

The positions 60° apart are known as the Lagrangian points. A French mathematician, J. L. Lagrange, first pointed out the stability of the positions in 1772. The 60° gap allows the smaller body to avoid destruction by the gravitational forces exerted by the larger one, and by the major body both are orbiting.

Shepherds in Orbit

Some of the small satellites, as we have seen, "shepherd" the planet's rings. The A Ring has a shepherd, Atlas. This tiny elongated body has a maximum diameter of 25 miles (40 kilometers). It

Did You Know?
Scientists studied Saturn long before the invention of the telescope. Records of the planet go back to 650 B.C. in Mesopotamia. Despite its great distance from Earth, the planet is visible to the naked eye as a bright star-like object.

keeps the fragments of the A Ring in order, giving the ring's outer edge a neat, sharp appearance. Satellites Prometheus and Pandora shepherd the F Ring. They orbit one on each side of it. They keep it distinct, and their gravitational influences probably cause the ring's "braided" effect.

The Voyager probes took as close a look as possible at the larger moons of Saturn, except for Phoebe, which was too far away to survey.

Mimas, only 242 miles (390 kilometers) across, is heavily cratered. One of its craters, Herschel (not visible here), is so large that the impact that made it must have come close to shattering the little moon.

Mimas is quite small. It has a diameter of 242 miles (390 kilometers) and orbits Saturn at a distance of 115,330 miles (185,600 kilometers). Its orbit, like those of all the other satellites except Phoebe, is synchronized with that of Saturn. Mimas rotates on its axis at exactly the same rate that it circles the planet, in just under an Earth day. It therefore keeps the same face turned toward Saturn at all times.

Close to Destruction

Mimas consists of at least 60 percent water ice and has a heavily pitted surface. Many of its craters are as

In this Voyager picture of Saturn, three moons show up distinctly. Enceladus is closest to the planet, with Tethys outside it. Top right is Mimas.

small as 1¼ miles (2 kilometers) across, but Mimas also bears the huge scar of a mighty impact that must have come very close to destroying it completely. Called the Herschel crater, it has a diameter of 80 miles (130 kilometers), almost a third the size of the whole satellite. In the center of the crater is a peak 3¾ miles (6 kilometers) high; on the opposite side of the satellite from the crater are enormous fissures which probably result from the same impact.

Did You Know?

In 1917, British astronomers observed Saturn passing in front of a star. They were able to record the way the star's light dimmed as the planet's rings moved across it. Variations in the dimming increased our knowledge of the structure of the rings and the gaps between them.

An artist's impression of Pioneer 11 after its encounter with Saturn in 1979. The Pioneer probes proved that it was possible for spacecraft to reach the outer planets without being destroyed by radiation or collisions with solid bodies.

Gleaming Enceladus

Enceladus is 310 miles (500 kilometers) across. It orbits Saturn at a distance of 147,950 miles (238,000 kilometers), once every 1·37 Earth days. It has a very smooth surface compared to the other satellites, a very high ice content, and an extremely bright, reflective surface, with an *albedo* of close to 100 percent. Enceladus has a very "young" geology. Some of its plains are almost empty of impact craters, which means that they have been formed within the last few hundred million years, during the last quarter of the moon's existence. The ridges and valleys that Voyager photographed on Enceladus seem to be the result of movements in the surface crusts.

Tidal Heat

The satellite Dione has a strong effect on Enceladus. Dione causes Enceladus to have a slightly elliptical orbit. When two or more conflicting forces, such as the gravitational pulls of two neighboring bodies, work on an orbiting body, they sometimes create what are called "tidal effects." The body being pulled in two directions at once sometimes changes its shape, and the energy of the opposing pulls can also create heat. Dione may be causing a certain amount of internal heating in Enceladus, which could result in molten material being forced out through faults in the crust.

Dione has a diameter of 695 miles (1,120 kilometers). Its density is 1·4 times that of water, which suggests that it has a higher rock content than its neighbor Tethys. Dione orbits Saturn once every 2·74 Earth days at a distance of 234,570 miles (377,500 kilometers). It has a surface of dark and bright contrasts, with dark patches outlined by bright streaks. It is possible that at one time Dione had an internal heat source, perhaps radioactive decay, which caused material to be pushed out on to the moon's surface.

50

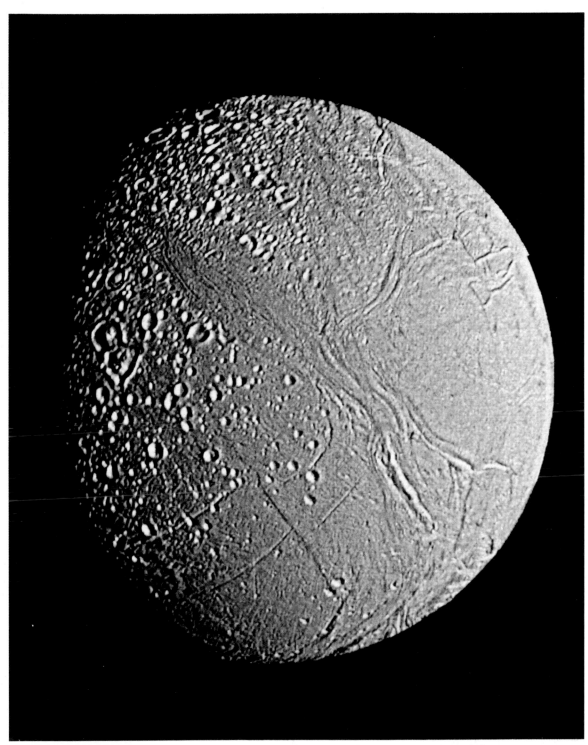

Opposite: This montage of photographs from Voyager 1 and 2 shows Enceladus in the foreground with Rhea at the lower right and Mimas, center right.

Above: Enceladus has the greatest reflectivity of any body in the Solar System. Its grooved terrain probably resulted from deformation of its crust while it was cooling.

Dione is seen here against the orange background of its parent planet. In addition to its craters, Dione has been found to have long, snaking valleys. They sometimes have borders of bright material, which could be the icy deposits left by released gases.

Icy Expansion

Tethys has a diameter of 650 miles (1,050 kilometers) and orbits Saturn once every 1·89 Earth days at a distance of 183,125 miles (294,700 kilometers). Consisting almost entirely of water ice, Tethys expanded as it froze during its long evolution. The added surface area formed a great trench, 62 miles (100 kilometers) wide and 3 miles (5 kilometers) deep, extending for almost 270° around the moon's sphere. This feature is called the Ithaca Chasma.

Tethys also bears the scar of an enormous impact, a crater 250 miles (400 kilometers) across. All of the surface features of Tethys seem to have been formed very early in the satellite's history.

Rhea

Rhea, with a diameter of 950 miles (1,530 kilometers) is second to Titan in size among Saturn's moons. Rhea takes 4·5 Earth days to orbit Saturn at a distance of 327,000 miles (527,000 kilometers). Voyager 1 came close to Rhea, passing it at a distance of less than 46,000 miles (74,000 kilometers). Its high-resolution photographs show an old, well-cratered surface.

Odd Moon Out

Hyperion, unlike the other named moons, is very irregular in shape, roughly 250 × 155 × 150 miles (400 × 250 × 240 kilometers) in size. Most elongated satel-

Opposite: Slanting down the lower portion of the pockmarked face of Tethys is a vast, trench-like valley 1,500 miles (2,400 kilometers) long, called Ithaca Chasma. It was possibly formed by a massive splitting of the moon's crust as the icy interior expanded.

lites adopt orbits with their length pointing toward the body they orbit. However, Hyperion's *long axis* is at an angle to Saturn. This fact, together with the satellite''s odd shape, suggests that it suffered a traumatic impact sometime in the relatively recent past. Eventually, it should adjust its position. Hyperion may even be a

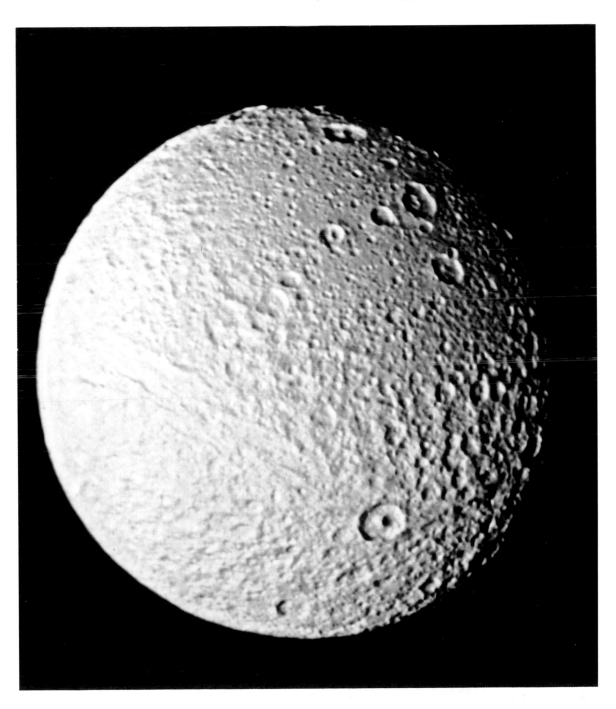

fragment left over from a collision. It orbits Saturn at a distance of 920,000 miles (1,481,000 kilometers) once every 21·28 Earth days. Hyperion has numerous irregular craters and resembles a dark cylinder.

Dark Matter

Iapetus takes more than 79 days to orbit Saturn at a distance of 2,213,000 miles (3,560,000 kilometers). This satellite has a diameter of 895 miles 91,440 kilometers). Although it appears to be made mainly of ice, it has distinctive dark markings which may be coal-like material from the satellite's interior. Iapetus may in fact

Voyager 2 took this photograph of Tethys 368,000 miles (594,000 kilometers) from its surface. Two distinct types of terrain are shown, a bright, densely cratered region and relatively dark, lightly cratered plains that extend in a broad belt across the satellite. The densely cratered terrain is believed to be part of the ancient crust and the lightly cratered plains are thought to have been formed by internal processes. A trough is clearly seen on the left hand side, an extension of the huge canyon system which extends nearly two thirds the distance round Tethys.

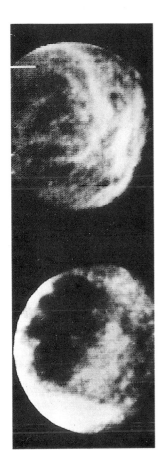

Above: These two images of Rhea were taken by Voyager from a distance of 1,180,000 miles (1,900,000 kilometers) and 1,680,000 miles (2,700,000 kilometers). Like Dione, Rhea displays bright streaks known as "wispy terrain," which may be deposits from released gases.

Right: Because of its high reflectivity – 60 percent – Rhea can be photographed with high definition. Voyager 1 took this from 46,000 miles (74,000 kilometers) away, shows details as small as 1¼ miles (2 kilometers) across. Rhea's cratering is very ancient; many of its craters now appear irregular in shape and are masked by a coating of rubble.

55

Right: A montage of images of the Saturnian system made up from images taken by Voyager 1. It shows Dione in the foreground, Saturn rising behind, Tethys and Mimas fading in the distance to the right, Enceladus and Rhea off Saturn's rings to the left and Titan at top right.

have a core of heavier material than the ice which is mainly in evidence.

Captured Loner

An artists impression of Saturn as it would be seen from Rhea. It shows the moon's icy and reflective surface. Rhea, next in size to Titan among Saturn's moons, is half ice, half silicate rock.

Most distant of all the named moons of Saturn, Phoebe is also the least known. It is small, with a diameter of only 125 miles (200 kilometers). It takes more than 550 Earth days to complete one orbit, at a distance of 8,047,000 miles (12,950,000 kilometers) from the parent planet. The Voyager images of Phoebe were

Iapetus is a two-faced moon, with a dark hemisphere toward the direction of its orbit, and a bright trailing hemisphere. The bright side reflects light from its ice, while the dark side seems to be covered in a rusty-black coating which may be made of a primitive carbon-containing substance.

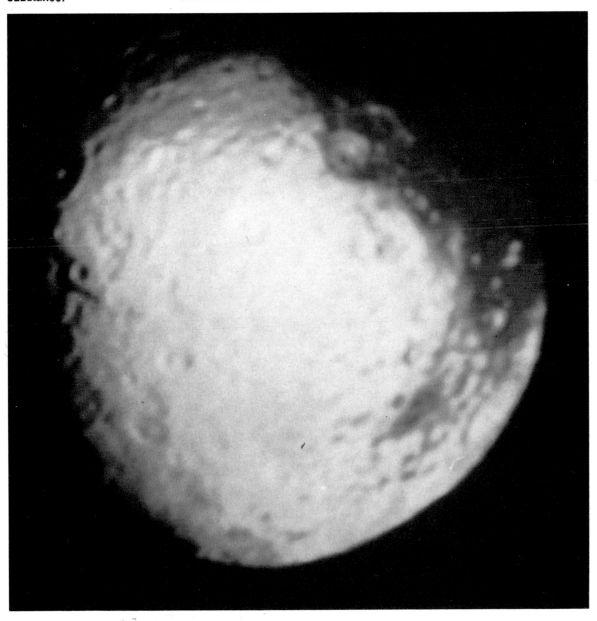

made at a great distance — over 1,367,000 miles (2,200,000 kilometers) away — and are vague and indistinct. Phoebe does not have a synchronous rotation, but rotates on its own axis about once every 9 hours. With its highly inclined orbital angle, retrograde motion, and great distance from Saturn, it is likely that Phoebe is an asteroid which has been captured by the planet.

Phoebe marks the outer boundary of the known satellite family of Saturn. It is as small as some of the unnamed satellites that have been discovered recently. It is possible that future spaceprobes will find more members of the family orbiting in the dark outer reaches. Some may follow or precede the larger moons at precise, ordered distances; others may "ride shot-gun" on the circling flocks of icy particles that make up the distinctive ring disk that marks Saturn as something special, even to amateur astronomers with simple telescopes here on Earth.

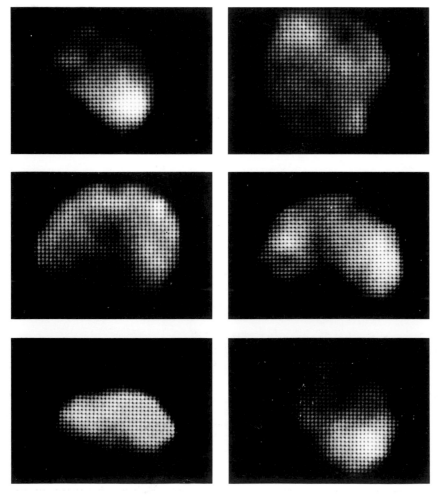

Phoebe is still a mystery moon. The Voyager mission was only able to photograph it from 1,367,000 miles (2,200,000 kilometers) away, providing a series of images showing its rotation. Phoebe, the outermost of Saturn's known moons, orbits the planet in a retrograde direction.

Books to Read

INTRODUCTORY READING:
Album of Spaceflight by Tom McGowen (Macmillan, 1987)
Believe It or Not Space Facts by David Baker (Rourke Corporation, 1987)
The Giant Planets by Alan E. Nourse (Franklin Watts, 1982)
Our Future in Space by Tim Furniss (Franklin Watts, 1986)
Rockets and Spaceflight by Myring (EDC Publishing, 1982)
Saturn by Dennis B. Fradin (Children's Press, 1989)
Saturn by Seymour Simon (Morrow Junior Books, 1985)
Saturn: The Ringed Beauty by Isaac Asimov (Gareth Stevens, 1988)
Saturn: The Spectacular Planet by Franklyn M. Branley
    (Harper & Row Junior Books, 1987)
Solids, Liquids and Gases by Jacqueline Barber (Lawrence Hall of Science, 1986)
Space Facts: Records-Lists-Facts-Comparisons by S. Reid (EDC Publishing, 1987)
Space Tour by Dan Mackie (Penworthy Publishing, 1986)
The Stars: From Birth to Black Hole by David J. Darling (Dillon Press, 1985)
U.S. and Soviet Space Programs: A Comparison by David E. Newton
    (Franklin Watts, 1988)

FURTHER READING:
The Far Planets by Time-Life Books Editors (Time-Life, 1989)
Far Travelers: The Exploring Machines by Oran W. Nicks (United States Government
    Printing Office, 1985)
Galileo by Stillman Drake (Oxford University Press, 1980)
Galileo and the Magic Numbers by Sidney Rosen (Little, Brown, 1958)
Interiors of the Planets by A. H. Cook (Cambridge University Press, 1981)
Introduction to Space: The Science of Spaceflight by Thomas D. Damon
    (Orbit Book Company, 1989)
Laws of Gases edited by I. Bernard Cohen (Ayer Company Publications, 1981)
Living Aloft: Human Requirements for Extended Spaceflight by Mary M. Connors (United
    States Government Printing Office, 1985)
A Photographic Atlas of the Planets by Geoffrey Briggs & Frederic Taylor
    (Cambridge University Press, 1986)
Protostars and Planets II edited by David C. Black & Mildred S. Matthews
    (University of Arizona Press, 1985)
Space Almanac by Anthony R. Curtis (ARCsoft Publications, 1989)
Space Medicine by Paul Rambaut (Carolina Biological Supply Company, 1985)
The Space Program Quiz and Fact Book by Timothy Benford & Brian Wilkes
    (Harper & Row, 1985)
Spaceshots: The Beauty of Nature Beyond Earth by Timothy Ferris (Pantheon, 1984)
World Atlas of Satellites edited by Donald M. Jansky (Artech House, 1983)

Glossary

ACHROMATIC (AND APOCHROMATIC) LENS A lens made up from two (three) different types of glass, which reduces chromatic aberration.

AIR TELESCOPE An early, very long type of refracting telescope which had no tube between the eyepiece and the objective lens.

ALBEDO The extent to which a body reflects light shining on it. It is the ratio of the amount of light reflected to that received.

APERTURE The diameter of the objective lens or primary mirror of a telescope.

CASSINI DIVISION A 2,500-mile (4,000-kilometer) wide gap between Saturn's A and B rings, discovered in 1675 by G. D. Cassini.

CHROMATIC ABERRATION False colors caused by the difficulty of bringing all colors to a single focus when viewing an image.

CO-ORBITAL Two or more satellites following the same orbit around their parent body are said to be co-orbital.

DOPPLER EFFECT The apparent change in sound or color or other radiation as an object approaches or recedes from an observer.

EQUATORIAL JET A powerful wind racing round a planet's equatorial region, usually at high altitude.

FOCAL LENGTH The distance between the lens or primary mirror and the point of focus of a telescope.

LONG AXIS The longest center line dissecting an irregular or elongated body or shape.

MAGNIFICATION Measurement of the strength of a lens.

MEAN DISTANCE The average distance of, for example, a planet following a non-circular orbit of the Sun.

MICROMETEORITE A particle of cosmic dust which is so small that it slows down when it enters an atmosphere and free-falls to the surface without heating up.

OBJECTIVE LENS The lens in a refracting telescope that is closest to the observed object.

OBLATENESS The flattening of a spherical body because of its rotation. It is measured by subtracting the polar diameter from the equatorial diameter and dividing the result by the equatorial diameter.

OPPOSITION The position of a planet when it is directly opposite the Sun as seen from Earth, that is, with Earth between the planet and the Sun.

PHOTOCHEMICAL SMOG Fog caused by the effects of sunlight on hydrocarbon emissions.

ROCHE LIMIT The minimum distance at which a satellite can maintain a stable orbit without being destroyed by tidal forces.

ZODIAC A band around the celestial sphere which was divided by ancient astronomers into 12 parts, or signs, representing constellations.

Looking at the Planets

Saturn can be difficult to find, because of its great distance from Earth. However, once you come across it, it is unmistakable. Saturn does not appear any more distinct than nearby bright stars, so the more powerful the telescope, the better, although you can see the rings plainly with a good pair of binoculars.

The rings show up best when they are tilted as we look at them. This happens once every 15 years, twice each 30-year orbit. They were at their most visible in 1988 and will be again in 2003. Between 1995 and 1996, the rings are edge-on to the Earth and hard to see. An almanac will tell you which sector of the sky to search, according to the year and season.

Saturn is at its brightest during opposition. When the rings are edge-on to Earth, conditions are best for finding Saturn's largest moons, Titan, Rhea, Thys and Dione, for which you will need at least a 2½ inch (60mm) refracting telescope

Index